EXPLORER BOOKS

VANISHED

by Jean Waricha

A TRUMPET CLUB ORIGINAL BOOK

Published by The Trumpet Club
1540 Broadway, New York, New York 10036

Copyright © 1993 Parachute Press, Inc.

ISBN: 0-440-83052-4

Printed in the United States of America
November 1993
3 5 7 9 10 8 6 4 2
CWO

PHOTOGRAPH CREDITS

pp. 7, 19, 23, 27: © UPI/Bettmann; *pp. 13, 15*: © Royal Geographic Society,
London; *pp. 30, 32, 40, 45, 48, 51, 52, 55*: © AP/Wide World Photos

Cover: Ambrose Bierce, © Culver Pictures; Amelia Earhart, © AP/Wide World
Photos; Michael Rockefeller, © AP/Wide World Photos; Agatha Christie, © UPI/
Bettmann

Contents

Introduction   **1**

1   Ambrose Bierce: The Perfect Ending   **3**

2   George Leigh Mallory: Disappearance
at the Top of the World   **10**

3   Agatha Christie: A Mystery Writer's
Best Mystery   **17**

4   Amelia Earhart: Lost at Sea   **25**

5   Michael Clark Rockefeller: Adventures
in the Jungle   **37**

6   D. B. Cooper: Parachuted into Thin
Air   **43**

7   The Bermuda Triangle: Invisible Door
to Another World?   **51**

Introduction

People are fascinated by mysteries, especially when they are true stories. Some people like to think that every mystery has a logical explanation—but does it? Sometimes things happen that we simply cannot explain.

This book tells the stories of seven mysteries that have never been solved. Six of them are famous cases of people who disappeared without a trace. At the age of 71, writer Ambrose Bierce went off to Mexico to join the army and never returned. George Leigh Mallory, a mountain climber, was trying to become the first man to reach the top of Mount Everest when he disappeared, never to be seen again. Agatha Christie, the famous mystery writer, was missing for ten days—and when she was found, she couldn't remember what had happened to her. Amelia Earhart was on her way to becoming the first woman pilot to fly all the way around the world when her plane vanished in the Pacific Ocean. D. B. Cooper hijacked a plane, demanded, and got, $200,000, and then parachuted to earth. He was never found. And Michael Clark Rockefeller, a young adventurer and son of one of the richest men in the world, went off to explore the wilds of New Guinea and disappeared. No amount of his father's money could find him and bring him back.

And then there is the seventh mystery: the famous Bermuda Triangle, a huge area of ocean where ships and planes—and the people inside them—have disappeared without explanation.

As you read these true stories, ask yourself what *you* think happened. Was Ambrose Bierce killed in a Mexican war—or did he kill himself? Did George Leigh Mallory ever make it to the top of Mount Everest—or did he die in a snowstorm or an avalanche before he got there? Did Agatha Christie set up her own disappearance to get revenge on her husband? Was Amelia Earhart just a pilot—or was she a spy? If D. B. Cooper jumped from the airplane did he survive? Did Michael Rockefeller drown, or was he killed by the natives? Is there a strange force under the sea at the Bermuda Triangle?

These are just a few of the many questions that have been asked. No one has been able to answer them. Now *you* are on the case. Good luck!

1

Ambrose Bierce

The Perfect Ending

Ambrose Gwinnett Bierce was born on a backwoods farm in southeastern Ohio on June 24, 1842. He grew up to be a famous West Coast writer and was known to be a mean, unpredictable man. He once wrote a short story called "A Strange Disappearance." But perhaps the strangest disappearance in his career was his own at the age of 71.

Bierce spoke very little about his unhappy childhood, except to call his parents "unwashed savages." His father was an unsuccessful farmer. His mother was a grim, stern woman. Neither parent showed any affection for the other or for their ten children.

Ambrose was the youngest child. All of his brothers and sisters had names beginning with *A:* Abigail, Addison, Aurelius, Amelia, Ann, Augustus, Andrew, Almeda, Albert.

When he was four, Ambrose's family moved to a farm in Warsaw, Ohio. Ambrose hated the endless chores and was constantly being beaten by his father for pulling pranks. The one place where Ambrose could escape his hard life was in his father's library. For a poor farmer, Ambrose's father had a large library. Ambrose read every book he found there.

At the age of 15, Ambrose left home and traveled east. He worked on an antislavery newspaper and studied engineering at the Kentucky Military Institute in Franklin Springs for a year.

In 1861 the Civil War broke out between the northern and southern states over the issue of slavery. Ambrose Bierce joined the northern side in the war against slavery. He signed on with a volunteer regiment as a private. Eventually he rose to the rank of first lieutenant and began making maps for his regiment. Mapmaking was very dangerous, since sketches of enemy territory had to be made while fighting enemy soldiers. At the battle of Kennesaw Mountain in Georgia, Ambrose was wounded in the head. It was some time before the bullet could be safely removed.

According to his brother Albert, Ambrose was never the same after he was wounded. Although he recovered physically, his outlook on life changed for the worse. Ambrose became a bitter man who always saw the worst in everyone and trusted no one. He became fascinated with terror and death.

After the Civil War, Ambrose traveled to San Francisco, where he got a job as a night watchman. During his free time he read, studied, and practiced writing. By 1866 he'd taught himself enough to get a job as a journalist.

He began by writing a column for a paper called the *News-Letter*. Ambrose made fun of life in California and mocked important local citizens. His writing was funny, but so nasty that he earned the nickname "the Wickedest Man in San Francisco." In one column he wrote about a woman who was suing the city after falling into a sewer. Ambrose wrote, "It is surprising that the lady decided to go to court. We would think that one adventure in a sewer would be enough for anyone."

Ambrose also began to write short stories—scary ones. As the author of stories such as "An Occurrence at Owl Creek Bridge" and "The Damned Thing," he was compared with the famous horror writer Edgar Allan Poe. His reputation grew, and Ambrose got a new nickname—"Bitter Bierce."

In 1871, Ambrose married, although he had often said marriage was only for fools. His wife, Mary Ellen Day, was the daughter of a successful San Francisco gold miner. She was attracted by Ambrose's good looks. He stood 6 feet tall, with bright blue eyes and long, reddish-blond hair.

Ambrose and his wife moved to England, where he wrote for magazines and published his first three books. In 1877 his wife and his two sons, Day and Leigh—both born in London—went to California for a visit. There Mrs. Bierce discovered that she was going to have a baby, so she didn't want to return to England. Ambrose came home to be with her, and their daughter, Helen, was born in California.

Though he came home to San Francisco, Ambrose spent little time with his family. He often stayed away for weeks at a time, living in hotels and writing. When he was home, he slept all day and wrote all night. He did a column for a magazine called *The Wasp*. As usual, he made fun of the local big shots, especially wealthy people and politicians. Ambrose's quick wit made him instantly popular.

In 1885, however, the magazine was sold. The new owner was angry at Ambrose for having written nasty things about him in one of his columns. Now he had his revenge. Ambrose was fired. And having insulted practically everyone in San Francisco, Ambrose soon found out that no one wanted to hire him. But then one day a young man came to Ambrose's door to offer him a job on the *San Francisco Examiner*. This newspaper was owned by a well-known family—the Hearsts.

"Did the Hearsts send you?" Ambrose asked.

"I am Mr. Hearst," answered the young man.

For the next 20 years Ambrose wrote two columns a week for William Randolph Hearst's *Examiner,* which became the leader of a national chain of newspapers. Ambrose Bierce had a steady job, a decent income, and a large audience of readers. He attacked government officials, millionaires, and leaders in religion and writing.

But his personal life fell apart. After years of neglecting his wife, he separated from her completely. Ambrose led a strange life during the years between 1887 and 1906. He bought a house in the woods outside San Francisco where he lived like a hermit and filled the house with pet toads and lizards. He rode his bicycle through the woods, talking to squirrels, snakes, and rabbits. Though his best writing came out of this period, he had to deal with tragedy after tragedy.

His son Day Bierce killed himself in 1889 after shooting someone in a fight over a woman. His younger son, Leigh, married a girl whom Ambrose disliked, and father and son had many arguments. Leigh

Ambrose Bierce sits peacefully under a tree.

began drinking. While out drunk he caught pneumonia and died soon after. Ambrose attended his son's funeral but refused to talk to Leigh's wife. He had the body cremated and kept the ashes on his desk in a cigar box. According to friends, he often flicked the ashes from his cigars into the same box.

In 1913, Ambrose began to think about his successes and failures. The genius that had brought him fame and fortune was starting to fade. He'd lost his wife and sons, and he felt that his daughter, Helen, was stupid. His sharp tongue had driven off most of his friends. For the people who admired his books he had only scorn.

Ambrose decided to go to Mexico. "Naturally it is possible—even probable—that I shall not return," he wrote to his daughter. "Strange things happen—and I am 71."

He was heading into a bloody war that had been going on since 1910. Revolutionary forces led by Pancho Villa and Emiliano Zapata were fighting the dictatorship of General Victoriano Huerta. Visiting Mexico was very dangerous, and Ambrose knew it. He wrote to a friend, "If you hear of my being stood up against a Mexican stone wall and shot to rags, please know that I think that's a pretty good way to depart this life. It beats old age, disease, or falling down cellar stairs."

Ambrose arrived in Mexico in December 1913 and managed to join Pancho Villa's army. On December 26, 1913, he rode 4 miles to the town of Chihuahua to mail a letter. He wrote to his secretary, saying that he would leave the next day with Villa's army for

Ojinaga, a city Villa was planning to attack. That was the last anyone ever heard from Ambrose Bierce.

But it was only the beginning of the strange rumors and stories about his disappearance. Some people said that Ambrose was killed in the battle and was put on the list of dead under the name A. Pierce. But there was never any proof that A. Pierce was really A. Bierce.

Another story had Ambrose's sharp tongue as the cause of his death. Several times he had argued with Pancho Villa, calling him a common bandit. Although it's true that Villa started out as a mountain bandit, he had become an important rebel general. Some people say that Villa ordered Ambrose out of his camp, then sent gunmen after the writer. Other sources claim that he died in front of a Mexican firing squad. Again, no proof or witnesses.

Years later it was claimed that Ambrose had actually killed himself and been secretly buried in his own backyard. Some of his friends said Ambrose frequently mentioned that he wanted the Grand Canyon to be his tombstone. They suggested that he shot himself in the head on the rim of the Grand Canyon, then tumbled down.

Perhaps the most unusual story claims that Ambrose got lost in the wild regions of southern Mexico. There he was captured by a tribe of primitive Indians who boiled him alive and kept his shrunken remains in a jar. Supposedly they worshipped his remains.

We may never know what became of him. But we do know that he loved to give his stories weird endings. Ambrose Bierce would probably have thought the ending to his life was perfect!

2

George Leigh Mallory
Disappearance at the Top of the World

Who was the first person to climb the world's tallest mountain? That secret may lie with the vanished explorer George Leigh Mallory, who disappeared in 1924 near the peak of Mount Everest. History records Sir Edmund Hillary and his guide Tenzing Norgay as the first men to reach the summit, in 1953. But if Mallory's body or his equipment are ever found, history may have to be rewritten.

George Leigh Mallory was born in England in 1886. He first became interested in mountain climbing in 1904 when the housemaster at his prep school took some boys to the Swiss Alps during one summer vacation. Young George went along because his friends were going. A gymnast and natural athlete, George found mountain climbing fun. After that summer he continued to climb, but climbing was just one of the many activities he liked to engage in.

Then, in his senior year at Cambridge University, George Mallory met Geoffrey Winthrop Young. For Geoffrey Young, mountain climbing was more than a sport—it was the most important thing in his life. He invited Mallory on an expedition to the Alps in 1909. From then on, Mallory was interested only in mountain climbing, and Geoffrey Young became his close friend, his teacher, and his inspiration.

Mallory took a job as a schoolteacher and often led his students on climbs in England. During World War I, he served as an officer in the British Army. In the two years after the war, he became well known as one of the best British climbers, able to lead groups to the top of difficult peaks.

Around 1920 a group of British climbers were planning a climb up one of the most difficult peaks in the world . . . Mount Everest. Mount Everest is the highest spot on the planet. It rises 29,028 feet, almost 5½ miles high, on the boundary between Tibet and Nepal. The southern slopes of the mountain fall in Nepal, while the northern slopes are located in Tibet.

In the summer of 1921 an expedition to climb Mount Everest was led by Colonel D. K. Howard-Bury. It was made up of four scientists and four climbers. Among them was George Leigh Mallory. They were accompanied by more than 20 porters, men who carried their gear, which included ice axes, tents, stoves, sleeping bags, ropes, food, and personal items.

The climbers set off from Darjeeling, India, and traveled through the tropical rain forests of Sikkim to the great plateau of Tibet. Then they had to hike 300 miles across cold, barren, windswept country to reach the northern slope of Mount Everest.

For three months the expedition scouted around the mountain, trying to find a path to the top. There were no maps, no roads, and no guides. They explored several possible approaches, but none led all the way to the crest of the mountain. At last, in September, the team reached a flat area at 23,000 feet, where they could see a clear route to the top.

But the weeks of searching for that route had weakened and exhausted the team. Mallory knew that it wouldn't be possible to reach the top at that time. A raging blizzard was coming down from the peak. He was worried about whether or not the tents could stand up to such fierce winds.

Also, the higher they climbed, the thinner the air became. Mallory and his party were constantly dizzy. Sometimes they nearly fainted from lack of oxygen. Above 20,000 feet the climbers needed several gulps of air to take a single step. Everyone agreed that they would have to turn back. But they had accomplished their goal—they had found a route to the summit.

The following year, in 1922, Mallory returned to Everest. This time he was a member of an expedition led by General Charles Bruce that included a team of five climbers. In April the expedition reached the Tibetan plateau, where they rested for two days before they attempted to climb to the summit.

Until then, no one had ever climbed higher than 24,000 feet. Some scientists believed that no one could survive at an altitude higher than 25,000 feet without oxygen tanks. To be on the safe side, Mallory and the other climbers had brought tanks along. Climbers carried the tanks on their backs, and a long tube ran from the tank to a face mask. They were awkward and heavy, and made climbing the icy slopes even more difficult.

After two weeks of difficult climbing, the 1922 expedition reached an altitude of 25,000 feet. They attempted to rush up the mountain without the bulky oxygen tanks and tubes, but they had to stop at 26,800 feet. When they tried again, this time with oxygen tanks, they had to turn back after reaching 27,300 feet. The expedition had now reached the highest altitude people had ever climbed.

Instead of ending the expedition, Mallory and several companions decided to try once more, with the oxygen tanks. One of the climbers, who was still recovering from frostbite, turned back. Another climber was

George Mallory (top row, second from left), Andrew C. Irvine (top row, first from left), and seven other men from the Mount Everest expedition of 1924.

carrying photo equipment as well as his oxygen and just couldn't go on. But Mallory, two other climbers, and 14 porters kept going—and headed right into a terrible avalanche. Tons of snow swept down the slopes of Mount Everest, killing seven members of the team. Mallory and the other survivors escaped being buried by "swimming" through the snow. But they were pushed 200 feet down the mountain, to the edge of a cliff. There was no question of going on. Once again Mallory was forced to give up.

In 1924, Mallory returned to Mount Everest for a *third* time. In spite of all the dangers he faced—bitter-cold temperatures, fierce winds that could blow a man off the mountain, the dizzying effect of thin air, dehydration, the blinding glare from the sun shining on the ice—Mallory believed that he could conquer Mount Everest. When asked by reporters why he kept going back to the most dangerous mountain in the world, he replied, "Because it is there."

In April, the third Mount Everest expedition began its climb. The climbers planned to set up a series of camps, each smaller than the next, housing fewer climbers. In May a terrible blizzard stopped the expedition from moving anywhere for a full week. Temperatures dropped to 50 degrees below zero. Several climbers suffered from frostbite.

In June, Mallory, a young climber named Andrew C. Irvine, and four porters reached an altitude of 26,800 feet. They set up a rest camp to plan their attack on the summit.

Mallory and Irvine were now almost alone, and close to exhaustion, but they had to make a run for the top

George Mallory and Andrew C. Irvine leave their camp for a final dash toward the summit of Mount Everest—never to return.

or else once again abandon their quest. On June 8 there was a sudden clearing around the summit. By noon, winds had swept away the clouds. The peak of Everest lay in clear view. Mallory and Irvine had only a 2,200-foot climb to the top. They were so close, and the weather was perfect. So on the morning of June 8, Mallory and Irvine began a final dash.

From lower down, a member of the expedition watched the two climbers through a telescope. They were visible at 28,277 feet, about 750 feet from the top. They looked like two black spots moving up the snow-covered slope.

Then a sudden cloud hid the mountaintop and the two men. They were never to be seen again.

The cloud turned out to be a mountain blizzard. The

next morning there was no trace of the two climbers. Expedition after expedition was sent out to find them. All that was ever found was an ice axe, far below the peak of the mountain.

Members of the 1924 expedition believed that both Mallory and Irvine reached the top, but were lost on the way down. Those who have tried to retrace Mallory's steps say that he had a good chance of making it to the top before the storm. And he had enough oxygen left to make the three-hour climb. Mallory may have reached the top just before the blizzard hit.

When a Japanese mountaineering team scouted Everest in 1979, some Chinese climbers from a 1974 expedition went with them. One of the Chinese climbers told the Japanese climbers that he had seen the frozen body of an "English" on his earlier climb. But the Chinese climber died in an avalanche before he could locate the body.

Did Mallory reach the top? We may never know. However, he did take a camera along. If that camera is found, we may finally discover what happened to Mallory—and know the truth about this disappearance at the top of the world.

3

Agatha Christie

A Mystery Writer's Best Mystery

More than 400 million copies of Agatha Christie's mystery novels have been sold around the world. But her greatest mystery stars Agatha Christie herself, and no one has yet managed to crack the case.

Agatha was born on September 15, 1890, in Devonshire, England. She was the youngest daughter of Frederick Alvah Miller, an American who lived in England, where he had met and married a beautiful Englishwoman—Clarissa Boehmer. Clarissa was a free spirit, an enchanting young woman who believed in ESP—extrasensory perception.

Agatha was a happy red-haired girl who lived a sheltered childhood. Her older brother and sister, Monty and Madge, were usually away at school. Agatha learned to play by herself. At the age of three she taught herself to read, and she loved to make up stories.

Agatha never went to school. Her mother had decided that education destroyed a woman's eyesight and ruined her brain. So Agatha ended up learning at home, where she studied only those subjects that interested her. She never bothered to learn the rules of grammar or spelling. She also took lessons in cooking, dancing, singing, and piano.

When Agatha was 11, her father died. Now she spent more time with her mother, becoming her constant companion. Often the two traveled to Paris. They even took a vacation to Cairo, Egypt. As a teenager, Agatha loved to go dancing and was popular with young men. She received several marriage proposals.

During her early twenties, Agatha began writing. First she tried poetry, then short stories. She also studied nursing in this period.

But it wasn't until World War I that she started writing mystery novels—and also found real-life romance. The beginning of her writing career was interrupted when she met Archibald Christie, a handsome young British Army flier, at a party in 1912. World War I broke out two years later. Agatha went to work in an English hospital. Archie flew off to France to fight with the Royal Flying Corps. While he was home on a three-day pass, Agatha and Archie were married on Christmas Eve in 1914.

Two days after the wedding, Archie returned to France. For two years Agatha worked as a Red Cross nurse in an English hospital. Some of that time was spent working in the hospital pharmacy, giving out medicine. It was there that she learned a great deal about poisons and drugs. This knowledge was very useful to her during her career as a mystery writer.

While working at the pharmacy, Agatha began to plot her first detective story. Years earlier, her sister Madge had challenged her to write one because the sisters enjoyed reading them. Now Agatha decided to meet the challenge. A neighbor who read the beginning of Agatha's first novel thought it was very good. He suggested that she send it to a book publisher.

By the time the war ended in 1918, Agatha Christie had her first mystery novel published. It was called *The Mysterious Affair at Styles.* She didn't earn a lot of money, but the publisher made a deal with her to write five more books. Agatha was thrilled. She would go on to write many famous novels, such as *Murder on the Orient Express* and *And Then There Were None,*

Agatha Christie and her pet terrier posed for this picture when she was a young woman in her early thirties, about three years before her disappearance.

and to create popular characters such as Miss Marple and Hercule Poirot.

She and Archie, who had returned from the war, settled down to a quiet family life. Agatha gave birth to a baby daughter. She bought a house in the English countryside, which she called Styles. In her free time she continued to write. But writing was just a fun hobby for her. Agatha was very happy, and she thought her happiness would last forever.

In 1926, Agatha's life changed dramatically. First her mother died, and she faced the difficult job of cleaning out the house where she had been raised. It was a terribly sad time, and she needed support and comfort from her husband.

But Archie was no help. He said he couldn't cope with problems that involved death or sickness. In fact, he left Agatha and went to live in an apartment in London. Agatha had to deal with everything by herself, and became more and more depressed. She cried constantly, couldn't remember how to start her car, and even forgot how to spell her own name.

When she returned to Styles from her childhood home, her husband told her he'd fallen in love with another woman and wanted a divorce. Agatha was shocked. She became more and more withdrawn. Several friends worried about her and about what she might do to herself.

Then, on December 3, a dark and stormy Friday evening, Agatha packed a bag, left her daughter in the care of her household staff, and drove off into the night. To all appearances she had vanished. This mysterious disappearance, which would last nearly two weeks, has never been completely explained—even to this day.

The next morning the police found Agatha's car at a place called Newlands Corner, an hour's drive from her home. The car had gone off the side of the road and was found with its headlights on in a ditch. There was no sign of Agatha. Archie was notified in London and immediately left for the scene.

By the time Archie arrived, all of London knew of Agatha's disappearance. Reporters were everywhere. Tourists arrived by the carload and took souvenir pictures of the car. There was such a crowd that vendors appeared, selling ice cream and coffee.

Scotland Yard organized a big search for Agatha. Police, reporters, and volunteers combed the nearby woods looking for clues to this mysterious disappearance. Airplanes circled overhead hoping to spot Agatha, alive or dead, from the air. Psychics were called in to help solve the mystery of the missing mystery writer. Even Agatha's pet terrier joined the hunt! He was given her glove to smell, and then taken on a three-hour tour of the countryside. The dog became exhausted and fell asleep. Nothing was found.

Nine days passed without a single clue. The police asked the public for more help. Fearing Agatha was dead, they set up a massive search to find the body. Newspapers called it "The Great Sunday Hunt for Mrs. Christie."

On Sunday, December 12, thousands of people gathered where the abandoned car had been found. Farmers brought tractors to clear the woods. Motorcyclists raced up and down forest lanes. Ponds were drained and searched. There was such confusion that two men in Sherlock Holmes capes and hats were nearly run over by all the traffic while examining footprints in the road with magnifying glasses. But when night fell, the police were no closer to finding Agatha.

People began spreading rumors. Some claimed that Agatha had been kidnapped and was being held for ransom. The kidnappers were demanding all the royalties from her books.

Another rumor stated that Agatha had disappeared on purpose, for a publicity stunt. She was writing a new novel, and it was about to be serialized in London newspapers. Her disappearance would sell more copies.

One of the wildest "explanations" was that she had killed herself because she couldn't think of an ending to her latest novel! Archie Christie was not amused by these silly rumors, or by the questions the police were asking. "They think I've murdered my wife," he told a friend at his office.

Just when everyone was ready to give up the search, a mysterious call came to the police, telling them that Agatha Christie was alive and staying at a resort hotel. The resort was in the town of Harrogate, 200 miles north of the spot where her car had been found.

Archie Christie rushed to the hotel. He waited in the lobby. To his complete surprise, Agatha came down the stairs and picked up a newspaper right in front of him —but didn't recognize him! It appeared that she was suffering from a complete memory loss. Archie took Agatha's hand and walked with her into the dining room. Now she appeared to know him, but only as an acquaintance.

They left together, and Agatha was taken to see a psychiatrist, a doctor who specializes in mental problems. He said that she had *amnesia,* memory loss due to stress. With the help of the psychiatrist, Agatha eventually regained some of her memory. But she never remembered leaving Styles, or driving her car, or how she got to the resort. She went to the spa, she

This picture of Agatha Christie at her typewriter was taken in 1946 when she was 55 years old. During her lifetime she wrote more than 80 mystery novels.

said, because she saw an advertisement for it in a railroad station. She was able to pay for her room because she always carried a hidden supply of cash in her purse. That was all she ever said about the incident.

Neither Agatha nor Archie discussed this episode publicly for the rest of their lives. They were divorced in 1928, and Agatha married an archaeologist named Max Mallowan. She barely referred to her disappearance in her autobiography and agreed to interviews only if the subject was never mentioned.

It seems that Agatha never really understood what happened, or why it happened. Twenty years later she saw another psychiatrist about the missing ten-day period in her life. If she found answers, we don't know them. She kept silent until her death in 1976.

Many questions remain unanswered. Why did she leave her car? How did she get to the hotel more than 200 miles away? Was her disappearance a publicity stunt, or did she really lose her memory? Was it an attempt to win Archie back? Or was it revenge? As a mystery writer, Agatha had to know her husband would be a prime murder suspect—especially since they had argued that morning.

Agatha Christie gave the world more than 80 mystery novels and hundreds of short stories, each with its own clever solution. But it seems her greatest mystery —her own—will never be solved.

4

Amelia Earhart

Lost at Sea

In 1937, Amelia Earhart was the most famous female pilot in the world. AE, as she liked to be called, had already flown solo across the Gulf of Mexico, crossed the Atlantic by herself, and flown alone 2,400 miles from Hawaii to California. Now she was planning a flight no woman had ever done. "I have a feeling that there is just one more flight in my system," Amelia said to a friend. "This trip around the world is it."

Amelia's words turned out to be terribly true. Her round-the-world flight *was* her last. On July 2, 1937, she set off from Lae, New Guinea, in a twin-engine airplane. That was the last anyone saw of Amelia and her one-man crew.

Amelia Earhart was born in Atchison, Kansas, on July 24, 1897. In those days there weren't even any airplanes. No one in the Earhart family could have imagined that Amelia would one day find fame as an *aviatrix,* as female pilots used to be called. When Amelia was 10, her aunt took her to see one of the newfangled "flying machines." Amelia was not impressed. She was more interested in playing with her sister, Pidge, climbing trees, and using the BB rifle her grandmother had given her.

In 1914, World War I broke out. Millions were wounded. In 1917, when Amelia was 20, she went to Canada as a nurse's aide for the Canadian Red Cross.

While working in a hospital in Toronto, Amelia went to watch some fighter pilots fly stunts. One flier decided to give the people watching from the ground a big thrill. He buzzed them, swooping close over their heads. Most people ran. But Amelia Earhart stood her ground as the plane came closer and closer. At that moment Amelia realized she had to fly.

"That plane talked to me," she later told her father. Then she asked for $1,000 for flying lessons.

Her family couldn't afford the lessons, so Amelia set out to earn the money. She worked at the post office, tutored children, and took photographs. And Amelia made a deal with an experienced stunt pilot, a woman named Neta Snook. Neta taught Amelia without asking for full payment beforehand.

Amelia earned her pilot's license in 1922. Back then, there were only 11 other women in the world with pilot's licenses. The Earharts had more money now, and with the help of her family, Amelia bought herself a bright yellow Kinner Canary airplane.

She flew in several airshows with her new plane. Amelia loved to try every flying trick she could imagine. She would purposely go into dangerous spins, make her plane stall out in midair, and practice emergency landings in all kinds of places. Amelia loved the feel of wind on her face, the smell of gas fumes, and the thrill of danger.

Amelia loved flying, and she also loved dressing up like a flier. She was tall, lean, and freckled, with short

Amelia Earhart poses with her husband, George Putnam, before taking off from Newark, New Jersey, 1931.

blond hair. She wore high leather boots, tight khaki pants, a leather helmet and goggles, and a knee-length leather coat. Since she wanted to look like an experienced flier, Amelia slept in her leather jacket and rubbed grease on the coat so it wouldn't look new and shiny.

Her career took off in 1928 when she met George Palmer Putnam II, whose family owned a large publishing company. Putnam not only married Amelia but also managed her career. He sponsored Amelia in several airshows, and as her fame grew, Putnam began to sell products with Amelia's name on them. There were Amelia Earhart leather flight jackets with airplane buttons, Amelia Earhart lightweight luggage, and an Amelia Earhart line of sturdy travel clothes.

When Putnam met Amelia, he was helping to arrange a trans-Atlantic flight that would be the first time a female passenger—Amelia—crossed the Atlantic Ocean by air. At that time only seven planes had successfully crossed the ocean, and no woman had ever made the trip.

On June 4, 1928, Amelia took off from Boston for England with two male fliers, on an airplane named *Friendship*. The plane weighed close to 5 tons and had *pontoons,* or boatlike skids, instead of wheels, so it could land on water. To make sure it could be found if lost, the *Friendship* was painted bright orange. The 2,000-mile flight took 20 hours and 45 minutes. Although she had only been a passenger, this adventure made Amelia Earhart famous.

Amelia, however, was not satisfied. She wanted to cross the Atlantic alone—a solo flight. At the time, only *one* man had done this. Charles Lindbergh had succeeded in crossing the Atlantic solo five years earlier. In 1932, Amelia, dressed in khaki riding pants, a silk shirt, and a brown scarf, took her toothbrush and a comb and climbed into the cockpit of her airplane. Fourteen hours and 56 minutes later she landed in Ireland. Amelia was awarded all kinds of honors for this brave flight. France gave her the Knight's Cross of the Legion of Honor, England made her an honorary member of the British Pilot Guild, and President Franklin D. Roosevelt invited her to dinner. After the dinner, Amelia and Eleanor Roosevelt, the president's wife, went for a midnight spin in Amelia's airplane. Both women wore their long evening gowns, and Amelia flew the plane in elbow-length white kid gloves.

In 1934, Amelia flew solo from California to Hawaii, and in 1935 she crossed the Gulf of Mexico alone. From 1935 to 1937, she spent most of her time lecturing at colleges and universities. But all the while she was planning to fly around the world at the equator. For Amelia this was the greatest challenge of her life.

To prepare for her round-the-world flight, Amelia bought a Lockheed 10-E Electra aircraft. This was the finest airplane in the world, state of the art for 1937. It had an all-metal body, could fly as fast as 210 miles per hour, and could travel 4,500 miles without stopping to refuel. Amelia had the plane stripped of its seats and added extra fuel tanks. In the cockpit, more than a hundred dials and levers were all hooked up to the latest equipment. An automatic pilot was installed, as well as a radio direction finder that would identify a signal and fly to that spot. There was also a two-way radio system.

In 1937, Morse code was considered the best way to send long-distance messages. But Amelia had never learned Morse. In fact, she knew very little about the newly developed radio-navigation system. This may be why Amelia asked an old friend, a pilot named Frederick Noonan, to come along as navigator.

Amelia Earhart began her flight around the world on May 29, 1937, taking off from Miami, Florida. She flew to Puerto Rico, Venezuela, Suriname (then known

29

Amelia Earhart and her navigator, Fred Noonan, during a stopover in Indonesia on their 1937 round-the-world flight. Not long after this picture was taken, they disappeared.

as Dutch Guiana), Brazil, and then across the Atlantic. After landing in Senegal, Africa, she flew to Karachi, India, then to Bwira in Indonesia, and to the island of Timor, then onward to Australia and New Guinea. It was now the end of June.

From New Guinea she had only 7,000 more miles to fly. But this was the roughest part of the journey—crossing the huge Pacific Ocean. Amelia's next stop was Howland Island. She had to fly 2,556 miles over open water to a speck of land 2 miles long and half a mile wide. Both Amelia and her navigator were exhausted. Still worse, Noonan, an alcoholic, had begun drinking, and more than once Amelia had to rely on her own instinct to steer a course.

The trip from New Guinea on July 1 should have taken about 18 hours. Fourteen hours into the flight, Amelia contacted the radio crew on the *Itasca,* a U.S. Coast Guard cutter stationed at Howland Island. All they could hear Amelia say was "cloudy and overcast." Eighteen hours into the flight, at 6:45 A.M., Amelia again made contact with the *Itasca,* saying her position was doubtful. She thought she was about 100 miles away and wanted the crew to take a bearing, to zero in on her radio. "I will make noise in microphone," she said.

Amelia whistled into her radio. But she didn't realize that she had to make the sound for at least two minutes for the ship to get a bearing on her. Amelia's whistle lasted only a few seconds. She waited, hoping that they would find her plane and tell her which way to fly. She could have used her radio direction finder, but for some reason she didn't turn it on. Perhaps

31

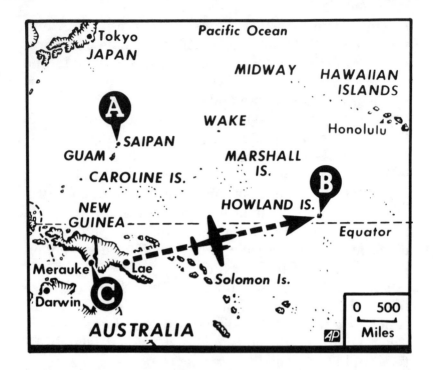

Amelia Earhart and Fred Noonan were flying from Lae, New Guinea, to Howland Island in the South Pacific when they disappeared forever, in July 1937.

Amelia didn't realize that the Coast Guard ship was sending out a homing signal.

At 7:42 A.M., Amelia Earhart's voice was heard again. "Cannot see you, but gas is running low." Then came silence.

Fifteen minutes later Amelia was heard again. "We received your signals but unable to get a minimum [a broadcast long enough to get a bearing]. Please take bearings on us and answer on 3,105 kilocycles." Again

Amelia was asking the Coast Guard ship to try and locate her and tell her which way to fly.

Then at 8:45 A.M. came a last message. Apparently Amelia was flying back and forth, north to south, looking for Howland Island. She was trying to tell the Coast Guard her position, but her reference, taken using the position of the sun, was very vague. The *Itasca* would have to cover hundreds of miles to find her plane.

Within hours of the last message a rescue mission was underway to find Amelia's plane. It was the largest search in history for one lost plane. Four thousand men in 10 ships and 65 airplanes searched the area for 16 days. They found nothing. Amelia Earhart and her airplane had vanished. The U.S. Navy gave up on July 12 after nearly two weeks of searching. They issued a statement that Amelia Earhart was "lost at sea."

The world was shocked. Almost immediately stories concerning Amelia's disappearance began to circulate.

One theory that became popular was that the flight around the world was just an excuse for her to fly over the Japanese-held Pacific Islands and photograph them. In only four years America and Japan would be fighting each other in World War II. The U.S. government knew the Japanese were using the Pacific Islands for military purposes and wanted to see what they were up to.

After the war, several eyewitnesses claimed that a pair of American pilots, one a woman, had been held on the island of Saipan. They had crash-landed in the Japanese-held area and were arrested as spies. But investigators were never able to prove whether or not the story was true.

Some people took this theory even further. Not only were Amelia and her navigator imprisoned by the Japanese, they claimed, but they were also rescued during the war and returned to the United States secretly, and were living in hiding.

In October 1991 a team led by Richard Gillespie set out to solve the Earhart mystery. Gillespie was the director of the International Group for Historic Aircraft Recovery. He believed that Amelia had made an emergency landing on Gardner Island, now called Nikumaroro, 1,600 miles southwest of Hawaii.

Gillespie spent months studying Earhart's last messages, as well as her flight plans. According to his calculations, Earhart and Noonan would have been flying in a direct line with Nikumaroro, since Nikumaroro is south of Howland Island, and Earhart was flying north to south.

In addition, Gillespie uncovered evidence that radio distress signals were picked up as far away as Honolulu, Hawaii, and Midway Island. The signals were heard for three days after the Earhart disappearance. Gillespie figured that these messages had to be coming from the area of Howland Island.

To Gillespie this meant Earhart had crash-landed somewhere and had been alive for at least three days. During that time she probably used the airplane generator as a means of sending the signals. After looking through naval files, Gillespie found that Nikumaroro had been searched only from the air. No expedition was ever sent there to investigate until Gillespie began searching.

Gillespie found a metal bottle cap, the heel of a woman's shoe, and a piece of scrap metal. These items, he claimed, proved Amelia Earhart died on Nikumaroro.

The bottle cap was made by the William R. Warner Company for a bottle of stomach medicine made in 1937. Amelia Earhart sometimes had stomach trouble and took this medicine.

The heel of the woman's shoe was identified as having come from a company called Cat's Paw. It fit a size-nine blucher-style oxford. This was the same size and type shoe Amelia Earhart wore.

The metal scrap seemed to come from the body of a pre–World War II airplane. It measured 23 inches by 19 inches and was made of a light aluminum alloy, or mixture of metals. This was the same sort of alloy as the metal in the plane Amelia used. The pattern of rivet holes in the scrap didn't match up to Amelia's Lockheed Electra. But repairs had been made to her plane during the trip. The piece of metal could have been added at that time.

Gillespie believes that these three artifacts support his theory that Amelia was on the island and survived the plane crash. But he doesn't know what happened to her. Nikumaroro had no fresh water supply and was inhabited only by crabs and turtles. Temperatures on the island reached as high as 120 degrees. Survivors of a crash-landing wouldn't have lasted long.

In spite of Gillespie's evidence, other experts are not

convinced that Amelia landed on Nikumaroro. They say there is no absolute proof that Amelia Earhart crashed on the island or died there. So the Earhart legend still remains . . . up in the air.

5

Michael Clark Rockefeller

Adventures in the Jungle

In 1961, Michael Rockefeller went to the remote islands of New Guinea, looking for adventure. He found more than he bargained for. When his boat capsized in a New Guinea river, Michael tried to swim ashore for help—and was never seen again.

Michael was not just another adventurer—he was the son of one of the richest men in the world. His father, Nelson Aldrich Rockefeller, was a politician. In 1958, Nelson was elected governor of New York State. He served four terms.

Michael was one of Nelson's five children. He was born in 1938 and went to Phillips Andover Academy, an exclusive prep school, and Harvard University. Those who knew Michael say that he was quiet, but had a rebellious streak. In college he liked to drive too fast and got a few speeding tickets. He spent his summers working—one in a supermarket in Puerto Rico and others on his father's ranch in Venezuela.

After graduating from Harvard, Michael intended to go to business school and eventually go into banking. But before he settled down into the life of a banker, Michael wanted to do something adventurous.

He served as an army private for six months. Then,

in March 1961, Michael joined an expedition to New Guinea organized by the Peabody Museum of Harvard University.

New Guinea is a country northeast of Australia made up of several islands. Dense jungle forest covers about 75 percent of the country, and the climate is hot and humid. The land is swampy near the coast. Inland there are steep jungle-covered mountains. The rivers and tides are swift and treacherous.

Several tribal peoples inhabit New Guinea. Most of them live primitive, simple lives as hunters or farmers. They grow yams, bananas, and *taro,* an edible root like a potato. From the jungle they collect wild fruits and nuts. Until recently these tribal peoples were headhunters and cannibals. Groups of scientists like those from the Peabody Museum often go to New Guinea to study primitive cultures. They make videos of the native people and collect examples of their tribal art.

The scientists from the Peabody Museum wanted to film the culture and songs of the New Guinea natives. Michael worked as a sound technician. But after six months of filming, the Peabody group was asked to leave New Guinea. Missionaries and officials complained that the scientists encouraged tribal warfare so they could capture it on film.

When the expedition left New Guinea in September, Michael returned to New York. But his home situation was not a happy one. His mother and father were divorcing after 31 years of marriage. It was a difficult time for Michael to be home, so within a week he decided to fly back to New Guinea. This time he wanted to collect native art.

On his first trip to New Guinea, Michael had become interested in the wooden carvings of the Asmat tribe. The Asmats carved wooden poles from mangrove trees to keep the memory of dead warriors alive. They also carved *soul ships,* dugout canoes with no bottoms. These "ships" would help the souls of the dead find rest.

Michael hoped to buy some of these carvings for the Museum of Primitive Art in New York, which was supported by the Rockefeller Foundation. He also hoped to buy other artifacts for the museum, including the skulls warriors painted and kept as trophies after killing their enemies.

On his second trip to New Guinea, Michael took with him Dr. Rene Wassing, a 34-year-old Dutch *anthropologist*—a scientist who studies different cultures—plus two native guides. The four men traveled along the coast in a 40-foot *proa*—two dugout canoes lashed together and powered by an outboard motor.

Michael Rockefeller was 23 years old. He had been in the army and was in great physical shape. He was 6 foot 1, lean and muscular.

The Asmat coast was very dangerous—full of muddy rivers, swamps, sharks, crocodiles, mosquitoes, and turbulent tides. The small expedition stopped in each village along the coast. They traded tobacco, cloth, and knives for primitive artifacts. Since Michael especially wanted the painted skulls, he offered ten steel hatchets for each painted skull. So many natives wanted the

Michael Rockefeller piloting a motorboat on a river during his first expedition to New Guinea with Harvard University, in 1961.

steel hatchets that they asked permission from government officials to go on just one more head-hunting raid to get skulls to sell him. Local government officials began to blame him for encouraging trouble and violence.

On November 16, 1961, Michael, Rene Wassing, and their two guides set off in their proa for the next village. When they were 3 miles offshore, a storm swamped the proa, ruined the outboard motor, and capsized the boat. The two guides swam for shore, which was so far away it could barely be seen. Michael and Wassing clung to the boat throughout the night. When morning came and no help arrived, Michael decided to swim to shore himself. He thought the two guides must not have reached the shore—or that they had not gone for help.

Michael tied two red 5-gallon gas cans together for a float. Then he tied his glasses around his neck, stripped to his shorts, and set off for shore.

Michael Rockefeller was never seen again.

Eight hours later Wassing was rescued by a Dutch boat. The two guides *had* reached shore and gone for help, but it had taken them almost a day to walk through the jungle to the nearest village. The New Guinea government began a massive search for Michael. Helicopters were used to search the area, along with 1,000 native canoes. A reward of 250 sticks of tobacco, a fortune to the natives, was offered to anyone who found Michael. Two thousand natives searched the coastline, but they never found a clue to Michael's disappearance.

Because New Guinea is so remote, it took three days

for Michael's father to get word that his son was missing. Nelson then flew to New Guinea with Michael's twin sister, Mary. Both Nelson and Mary spent hours flying over the area in a helicopter looking for some trace of Michael. Finally, after ten days of searching, Nelson Rockefeller held a news conference and called off the search. He and Mary flew home to New York.

No trace of Michael Rockefeller was ever found. One red gas can was eventually discovered far out to sea. But there is no proof that it was one of the two used by Michael. It is believed that Michael died swimming to shore—killed by sharks or crocodiles, perhaps, or drowned in the swift current.

Government officials weren't so sure. They believed that Michael, being a strong swimmer, probably made it to shore and then lost his life in the jungle. It wasn't until three years later that Michael was officially declared dead.

In December of 1972 an Australian sailor named Roy Hogan who had spent time in New Guinea claimed that Michael *did* make it to shore, where he was captured by the Asmat natives. Hogan was sure he had seen Michael alive—a blond man wearing glasses, living with the Asmats. The story was investigated but led to no trace of Michael Rockefeller.

We will probably never know for sure whether Michael drowned at sea, perished in the jungle, or made a secret new life for himself—far away from home.

6

D. B. Cooper

Parachuted into Thin Air

On November 24, 1971, an unlikely new hero entered American folklore. He was called D. B. Cooper, and his incredible getaway with $200,000 made history.

It was the day before Thanksgiving, and 24 passengers climbed aboard Northwest Orient Flight 305 heading from Portland, Oregon, to Seattle, Washington. One passenger, who gave the name of Dan Cooper, was about to carry out the only successful hijacking ever of an airplane inside the United States.

Dan Cooper—later known as D. B. Cooper because of a reporter's mistake—had bought his ticket with cash. He wore a business suit and carried a briefcase. To the flight attendants Cooper looked like an ordinary passenger traveling home for the holidays.

The takeoff went without problems. Cooper sat in the back of the plane. As the attendants began to serve drinks, Cooper handed one of them a note, which she pocketed without reading. Cooper anxiously got the attendant's attention and nodded for her to read it. The note said that he had a bomb in his briefcase and would blow up the plane unless his demands were met. He wanted $200,000 in $20 bills, and four parachutes brought onto the plane after it landed in Seattle.

The attendant immediately told the pilot, Captain William W. Scott, about the note. At first Captain Scott thought it was some kind of joke. But when Scott went to the back of the plane, Cooper opened his briefcase. Inside were two red cylinders with wires attached to a clock. Captain Scott now believed that Cooper was carrying a bomb.

The pilot notified the airport in Seattle, who then called the FBI and airline executives. The decision was made to give Cooper what he wanted.

Four parachutes were assembled from a nearby skydiving school. Then 10,000 $20 bills were collected from a Seattle bank. The FBI recorded the serial numbers from the bills before putting them into a canvas bag. They made a bundle that weighed 20 pounds.

When everything was ready, the plane landed at the Seattle airport. Cooper allowed the passengers to leave, but forced one flight attendant to stay. The FBI believed Cooper did this to make them think that he was going to have someone jump with him. It was his way of making sure the FBI wouldn't tamper with any of the parachutes.

After all the passengers left, the flight attendant walked down the stairs and picked up the money and parachutes. Cooper looked at each chute, then told the captain to ready the plane for takeoff.

Before Cooper allowed the plane to take off, he gave the pilot several instructions. First, the plane was to head for Reno, Nevada. But Captain Scott was not to fly above 10,000 feet. To insure this, the plane was not to raise its landing gear after takeoff. It appeared that Cooper had carefully planned and researched his getaway. A parachute jumper could not survive a jump from an airplane flying at normal altitude or speed. But the Northwest Orient airliner was a Boeing 727, which can stay in the air at much slower speeds than most jets.

The 10,000-foot limit had another purpose. That's the height at which airlines pressurize their planes' cabins. Cooper instructed Captain Scott *not* to do that. If the cabin were pressurized, the captain could have opened the cabin door, and Cooper might have been sucked out of the plane or knocked unconscious in the rush of higher-pressure air escaping the cabin.

These sketches of D. B. Cooper were made based on descriptions given by passengers and crew who flew aboard the airplane Cooper hijacked in 1971.

The plane took off. Two air force jets tried to follow it, but could not fly at such a low altitude or slow speed. Cooper ordered the attendant into the cockpit, then locked the door.

No one knows exactly what happened next. But ten minutes into the flight the captain noticed a red light on his control panel. This signal meant that a rear door had been opened, letting down an emergency-escape ramp. Minutes later the captain felt a "bump" in the plane, as if someone had jumped out. Later, in a re-creation of the event, the captain identified the same "bump" when a 200-pound weight was thrown from the back cabin door of a flying plane. So the captain and the FBI were convinced that a man had parachuted out of the plane. But what happened to the money? What happened to Cooper? No one knows.

The FBI launched a massive manhunt. Based on their re-creation of events, they knew that Cooper had parachuted out and landed somewhere near the Oregon-Washington border. Police and federal agents searched the area, helped by 400 army troops. They were joined by hundreds of tourists who were fascinated by the story of Cooper's disappearance. Some admired his skill and courage—and hoped to find the money! Cooper became a national phenomenon.

"Dan" Cooper now became "D. B." Cooper, thanks to a story by a national news-service reporter. The FBI was checking all male Coopers who lived in Portland just in case the skyjacker was using his real name. There was a D. B. Cooper who fit the description of the man on the airplane, and somehow a reporter found this out and wrote up the story. As it turned out, this

D. B. Cooper had moved out of town and was *not* the Dan Cooper who had held the flight hostage.

When weeks of searching turned up no new clues, the FBI agents gave up. Most of them believed that Cooper had to be dead. After all, he had bailed out of an airplane flying at an altitude of 10,000 feet wearing only a business suit and loafers. The weather that night had been inhospitable. The temperature was below zero, and a freezing rain was falling. He would have been battered by 200-mile-per-hour winds, and there was an excellent chance of his falling into Merwin Lake, Washington.

Months went by. Then on February 10, 1972, magazine writer Max Gunther received a letter from D. B. Cooper offering to sell his story for cash. Gunther feared a hoax, but got another letter and then a telephone call from the man who said his name was Dan Cooper—the name originally used to buy the skyjacker's ticket. Gunther began to think he might be dealing with the real thing. Unfortunately, after talking with another publisher, the "Dan Cooper" who was making the calls apparently got scared off.

In 1974 an escaped convict named Richard Floyd McCoy was killed in an FBI shootout in Pennsylvania. Unfortunately for McCoy, he'd left clues that led the FBI to his hideout. He had been an Army Special Forces helicopter pilot, and was serving time for skyjacking a United Airlines plane on April 7, 1972. McCoy's method was exactly like the one used by D. B. Cooper. In fact, comparing McCoy and a drawing of Cooper show that the two men look exactly alike. Although McCoy never admitted to being D. B. Cooper,

Part of the money that was paid to D. B. Cooper in 1971 was found in Oregon in 1980 by an eight-year-old boy during a family picnic!

some FBI agents believed that Cooper and McCoy were one and the same, but they had no proof.

The next break in the case happened on February 10, 1980. An eight-year-old boy named Brian Ingram found a bundle of $20 bills by the banks of the Columbia River near Portland, Oregon, while on a family picnic. The FBI later matched the serial numbers on the bills with ones given to D. B. Cooper. A second search was started, but nothing else was ever found.

Then in 1982, more than 10 years after the skyjacking, Max Gunther got another phone call. This time it wasn't D. B. Cooper but a woman who called herself Clara. Over several weeks, Clara told Gunther an unusual story.

According to Clara, who lived in a small town in the state of Washington, she found a man with a broken ankle hiding in a shed on her property on November 26, 1971. She knew, of course, that he was D. B. Cooper, but she did not turn him in. Instead, she fell in love with him and nursed him back to health. During this time, Cooper told her that he had hidden the money in the forest. When the two went back to find it, they discovered that animals had dug part of it up and dragged it away. They recovered only $103,000, most of which they were afraid to spend.

Clara said that they had a happy life together until Cooper became sick. According to Clara, he died in 1982. She contacted Max Gunther because she wanted the real story to come out. It was published, but her real name was kept a secret because she had helped a criminal get away with a crime.

Is this story fact or fiction? We may never know.

But millions of people all over the world know about D. B. Cooper. Books were published, a movie was made about him, and a song was written telling his story.

Even now, more than 20 years after his crime was committed, people gather each year in the little town of Ariel, Washington, on November 24. Ariel had served as the headquarters for the FBI search. Now the town celebrates D. B. Cooper Day. People come dressed in suits and wearing sunglasses—they even carry money bags. If they wish, they can join the D. B. Cooper Club.

D. B. Cooper has become an American folk hero. He's "The One Who Got Away."

7

The Bermuda Triangle
Invisible Door to Another World?

In the Caribbean Sea there is a place where thousands of people have disappeared. It's called the Bermuda Triangle. Why have so many planes, ships, and people

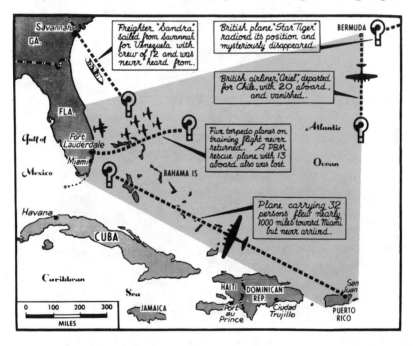

Savannah, GA.

Freighter "Sandra" sailed from Savannah for Venezuela with crew of 12 and was never heard from.

British plane "Star Tiger" radioed its position and mysteriously disappeared.

BERMUDA

British airliner "Ariel" departed for Chile, with 20 aboard, and vanished.

FLA.

Gulf of Mexico

Fort Lauderdale

Miami

Five torpedo planes on training flight never returned. A PBM rescue plane with 13 aboard also was lost.

Atlantic

Ocean

BAHAMA IS.

Havana

Plane carrying 32 persons flew nearly 1000 miles toward Miami but never arrived.

CUBA

Caribbean

Sea

HAITI

DOMINICAN REP.

Port au Prince

Ciudad Trujillo

San Juan

PUERTO RICO

JAMAICA

0   100   200   300

MILES

simply vanished there—never to be seen again? Why hasn't anyone been able to unravel its mystery?

The Bermuda Triangle runs from Bermuda to Puerto Rico to Florida and back. The baffling events that began there started in 1918 with the disappearance of a naval vessel named the U.S.S. *Cyclops*. World War I was in its final year. The 542-foot long cargo ship was on its way from Brazil to Baltimore, Maryland, carrying metal to make naval guns and propellers. But on March 5, 1918, the *Cyclops* made radio contact for the last time. Then the 19,000-ton

In 1918 the U.S.S. Cyclops *became the first of many ships to disappear without a trace in the Bermuda Triangle.*

ship carrying 309 crew members and passengers simply vanished.

It was the story of Flight 19, however, that made the Bermuda Triangle famous. On December 5, 1945, five small airplanes took off from Fort Lauderdale Naval Air Station for a routine training mission. It was 2:10 in the afternoon. The weather was clear. The mission was to take about two hours. All five airplanes were to fly a triangular route out over the Caribbean, then fly back to base.

But an hour and 45 minutes into the flight it was obvious that something was terribly wrong. The pilot of one of the planes radioed the tower. "I think we are lost," he said. "I can't see land. We must be off course."

The people in the tower were surprised. "What is your position?" they asked.

"I'm not sure. Everything's gone wrong. This is very strange."

Everyone in the tower was silent. What could be happening? How could they be lost? Wasn't the pilot's compass working? The people in the tower tried to contact the other pilots, but they also were lost and confused. None of the pilots could say exactly where they were, and they sounded panicky.

The people in the tower couldn't figure out the location of the five planes because the radio signals from the planes were too weak. As the hours passed, the radio signals only became weaker.

At 7 P.M. the tower heard a final message from one of the pilots. He repeated that he was lost. Then his radio went dead.

Darkness was falling, and a storm was brewing. The planes could only stay in the air for another hour before they would run out of fuel. The tower sent out rescue planes to find the missing aircraft and their crews. Within an hour, the rescue planes reached the area where the training mission was supposed to be. But there was no evidence of the five planes of Flight 19.

"No sign of the planes," a pilot from one of the rescue planes reported to the tower. "No wreckage."

Then, suddenly, the radio signal was lost. The rescue plane, along with its crew of 13 highly skilled men, was never seen or heard from again. It, too, had disappeared.

Now the people in the tower were very worried. A long and thorough search of the area by plane and boat followed, but no wreckage or crew members were ever found. Nothing. Everyone had just vanished.

A researcher and pilot named Lawrence David Kusche became interested in the mysterious disappearance of Flight 19. He believed that the mystery could be explained.

Kusche pointed out that the pilots and crew on Flight 19 were inexperienced. Most of them were trainees, just learning how to fly. The flight leader did have flying experience. But he had only recently moved to the Fort Lauderdale area. He was completely unfamiliar with the area they were flying over.

When his compass did not work, the flight leader kept changing direction, hoping to spot land. Kusche thought that since the flight leader really was on

This picture of the lead plane from Flight 19 was taken on June 26, 1945, at the Fort Lauderdale Naval Air Station, five months before the plane vanished. (The men pictured here are not those who were lost during the final flight.)

course, when he changed course he was actually flying *away* from land.

The flight leader also failed to switch his radio to an emergency channel. If he had, he probably would have been able to talk to the tower operators.

Why didn't he? Kusche suggested that the flight leader did not use his emergency channel because he did not think that the situation was dangerous. For some reason the flight commander, as well as the tower operators, did not seem to realize how much danger the pilots were in. They felt sure the planes would eventually get back on course and land safely. But they were wrong.

The pilots were probably forced to land in the water, Kusche said. But landing an airplane on a dark, stormy night in rough seas was too difficult for the trainees. All the planes were lost at sea.

But Kusche was unable to explain *every* mystery concerning the disappearance of Flight 19. Why did the compass fail? And what happened to the wreckage of the airplanes?

Flight 19 is only one of many unexplained disappearances in the Bermuda Triangle.

On January 7, 1958, millionaire Harvey Conover vanished into the Bermuda Triangle. Conover was the publisher of *Yachting Magazine* and considered to be one of the best sailors in the world. He had sailed his 45-foot yacht all over the world. He and a crew of three disappeared without a trace.

The *Marine Sulfur Queen,* a 425-foot freighter, disappeared in February 1963 along with a crew of 39. In January 1967, three disappearances occurred within the space of a few days. First a World War II *glider,* an aircraft without an engine, that uses airflow to fly, vanished into the Triangle with four people on board. Then two more planes—each carrying four passengers —disappeared. Extensive searches were carried out. They found no wreckage. No bodies. No clothes. Nothing!

In March 1973, the 20,000-ton freighter *Anita* set sail from Virginia to Germany with a cargo of coal.

Neither the ship nor its crew were ever heard from again.

The mystery continued. Airline pilots as well as boaters were warned about the dangers of the Triangle. Some people wanted to close off the area to sea and air traffic. Others said that all the disappearances could be explained by such things as pilot error or bad weather.

These are only a few of the many odd occurrences in the Bermuda Triangle. People have thought up all kinds of strange theories to explain its mysteries. One of the strangest is that the Triangle is a loading station for aliens. Some people say that aliens landed a space station in the area long ago. These alien beings capture boats and planes, as well as their passengers. Then the aliens fly the earthlings off to their planets, where they study them. There is no scientific evidence to support this theory—though many people *have* reported UFO sightings in the area.

Other people think that under the Caribbean Sea is an invisible door to another world. Once you fall through the door, there is no return.

But some scientists say that they can logically explain the disappearances in the Bermuda Triangle. In that area, they say, many parts of the ocean bottom are covered with quicksand. If a plane or ship ran into trouble there, the wreckage could vanish forever in the quicksand.

Other parts of the Triangle's ocean bottom are made up of limestone mountains. Deep caves are located in these mountains. The currents in the caves are so strong that they create whirlpools on the surface. And these whirlpools are so powerful that they can suck small planes or ships into the caves.

Then there are *waterspouts*—powerful whirlwinds of water whipped by strong winds—and tidal waves. A small airplane flying into a waterspout would be torn apart. A small boat caught in a tidal wave could be capsized and sunk. And what about the wreckage? It could vanish in the underwater caves or quicksand.

But what about the messages from pilots reporting compasses gone wild or failed radios? Some boat captains have even said that the batteries on their ships have gone dead when they were passing through the area.

Some scientists think that this mystery can be explained as the result of strange magnetic forces in the Bermuda Triangle. These forces could make electrical equipment fail or even make compasses spin. But what would cause the unusual magnetic forces? One scientist has stated that they could be the result of a meteorite from outer space which landed in the Bermuda Triangle long, long ago.

These theories concerning the disappearances in the Bermuda Triangle offer some explanation but fail to answer all the questions. Why were there few distress calls or sightings of bad weather? And the presence of quicksand does not fully explain why no wreckage at all has been found. Why were there no oil slicks, pieces of wood, or life rafts visible? Some small bits of evidence should have floated to the surface.

Is there really something strange about the Bermuda Triangle—something supernatural? Unless these questions are answered, we may never know. The Bermuda Triangle has been a mystery for years—and it remains one to this day.

Other titles in the Explorer Books series

BATS

BEARS

DISASTERS

FIRE

GREAT APES

HAUNTED HOUSES

JUNGLES & RAIN FORESTS

MAN-EATERS

MUMMIES

OWLS

POISONOUS CREATURES

POLAR BEARS
AND OTHER ARCTIC ANIMALS

SECRET CODES

SHARKS

TREASURE

WHALES & DOLPHINS

WOLVES